Talk Talk

Effective Communication
in Everyday Life

T0162970

Talk Talk

Effective Communication
in Everyday Life

Mavis Klein

**PSYCHE
BOOKS**

Winchester, UK
Washington, USA

First published by Psyche Books, 2013
Psyche Books is an imprint of John Hunt Publishing Ltd., Laurel House, Station Approach,
Alresford, Hants, SO24 9JH, UK
office1@jhpbooks.net
www.johnhuntpublishing.com
www.psyche-books.com

For distributor details and how to order please visit the 'Ordering' section on our website.

Text copyright: Mavis Klein 2012

ISBN: 978 1 78099 882 4

A CIP catalogue record for this book is available from the British Library.

Design: Stuart Davies

Printed and bound by CPI Group (UK) Ltd, Croydon, CR0 4YY

We operate a distinctive and ethical publishing philosophy in all
areas of our business, from our global network of authors to
production and worldwide distribution.

CONTENTS

By the Same Author

Lives People Live: A Textbook of Transactional Analysis
How to Choose a Mate
Discover Your Real Self
Understanding Your Child
Pain & Joy in Intimate Relationships
Live Issues: Reflections on the Human Condition
The Psychodynamic Counselling Primer
Teach Yourself the Psychology and Astrology of Human
Relationships
Being a Therapist: A Practitioner's Handbook

Foreword

This book is about making the most and the best rather than the worst and the least of our everyday interactions with other people.

Most people's everyday lives involve regular interactions with line managers, subordinates and peer group colleagues, and even those who are self-employed are inevitably involved with others in the pursuit of their work.

While the aim of this book is primarily to elucidate the nature of all our human interactions, however fleeting, it is hoped that readers will find in it illumination of aspects of their more intimate relationships as well.

The language used is the vivid and easily understood vocabulary of Transactional Analysis and, for those who are interested, the Appendix offers an overview of this theory.

Chapter One

Strokes

What is a Stroke?

People give and receive strokes from each other every time they do or say anything that acknowledges the other's presence. Any intentional body contact made with another person is a stroke, but so, too, are words and many other symbols that show we are aware of the other person. Thus a smile, a frown, a telephone call, an invitation, a thank-you note, or a threat are all received as strokes, as well as pats on the arm, smacks, kisses or kicks. Strokes vary in their intensity and value, from the most highly praised 'I love you' to the very slightly valued nod of recognition from a passing acquaintance.

We need strokes in our daily lives as much as we need food, in order to survive. And, indeed, in the earliest months of our lives, we need strokes in the most basic sense of skin to skin contact. This was definitely discovered during World War II in Paris, where there was an orphanage in which apparently well-fed and well-cared for babies were losing weight and wasting away and dying, for no discernible reason. A psychiatrist called René Spitz was called in to investigate, and he discovered that the reason for these babies dying was that the staff were so busy feeding and keeping clean the babies in their care that nobody had any time to pick them up and cuddle them. And so it has become received wisdom that the intimate skin-to-skin contact that a baby has with its primary caretaker – usually its mother – is as vital to the baby's survival as the milk it is fed.

René Spitz's finding was supported by the famous experiments of the behavioural psychologist Harry Harlow who, in the 1950s, housed orphaned monkeys in a cage containing two monkey-shaped surrogate mothers: a wire mesh one to which was attached a feeding bottle, and a soft cloth one without any feeding bottle. The baby monkeys spent far more time clinging to the cloth than to the wire surrogate, and they invariably ran to the cloth one whenever they were startled by a loud noise.

In the light of this knowledge, Eric Berne, the founder of Transactional Analysis, asked himself, if physical strokes are so imperative a need in infancy, how do we manage without them once infancy is passed? He decided that we do, indeed, go on needing strokes throughout our lives, on a daily basis, in exactly the same way and as imperatively as we go on needing food. However, Berne decided, once the period of infancy is over, we learn to value symbolic substitutes for skin-to-skin contact, including any eye to eye contact we make with another human being.

The first symbolic stroke that we are capable of appreciating – and returning – is our mother's smile, when we are about six weeks old. And then, as we grow up, we learn to value a multitude of other symbolic strokes - gifts we are given, birthday and Christmas cards, invitations to parties ...We 'say it with flowers' and in innumerable other ways.

Everything that can be said about strokes is precisely analogous to what we may say about food.

Although we go on throughout our lives having our stroke needs met largely symbolically, at the deepest level of our beings, we all yearn for the nirvana we once experienced, ideally, at our mother's breasts. Loving sexual intercourse is the closest we ever get to that nirvana (ambrosia) again, and so is the most highly valued experience that life has to offer us.

There have been some experiments done to find out how long people can manage without strokes. In one experiment, some normal, healthy adults were put in a situation where they had no contact of any kind with another human being, for as long as they could bear. What would you guess was the longest time that anybody could manage? After 36 hours there was nobody left who didn't feel they were going out of their mind (which, interestingly, is about the same length of time that most people can go without food before becoming desperate). And, as we all know, solitary confinement is the most horrible punishment that can be inflicted on people, because it is a situation in which they are completely stroke-starved. While there are constitutional differences between people in how long they can survive without food or water, stroke-deprivation is a sanity – if not life- threatening situation for nearly everybody.

Different Kinds of Strokes

All strokes are *positive* or *negative* and *conditional* or *unconditional*. Positive strokes make us feel good about ourselves; negative strokes make us feel bad about ourselves. But we would rather have negative strokes than no strokes at all and, quite rightly, just as nobody who was starving would be foolish enough to refuse a McDonald's and coke if there was no other food available. So those people who, for whatever reason, can't get positive strokes will choose negative strokes rather than none at all.

By and large, the only truly *unconditional positive strokes* people ever receive are from their mothers and fathers. And, if we are lucky, we can rely on our parents to go on loving us throughout their lives, no matter what we ever do or say. Unconditional positive strokes say, 'I love your existence. No matter what you do, I will always love you.'

Unconditional negative strokes are given instead of unconditional positive strokes to some unhappy people, even in infancy. These strokes effectively say, 'I hate you and wish you didn't exist. There's nothing you can ever do to please me or to make me love you.' Those people in the world who were effectively brought up on unconditional negative strokes spend their whole lives, however unconsciously, looking for the unconditional positive strokes they were entitled to from their parents, but never got. They are likely to have many self-destructive propensities. And there are other, less disturbed people who, nevertheless, having been given a surfeit of unconditional negative strokes as children, are likely to reach out pre-emptively and with great vigour towards every new person they meet, in the hope that this is the one who will give them the infantile, unconditional positive strokes they were deprived of. They are inclined to see somebody across a crowded room and say, 'Ah, I'm in love with you. I knew the moment I saw you that you're the person I've been waiting for all my life;' and then the whole thing blows up in no time at all, because they provocatively test the unconditionality of the other's love with their own bad behaviour, and quickly find – of course – that there are limits to the other's love. Eventually, it is to be hoped, such people are able to acquire the insight to realize and accept, with rational resignation, that they are never going to get those unconditional strokes of which they have been deprived, but that *conditional positive strokes* are well worth having.

Conditional positive and *conditional negative strokes* are the usual strokes that are on offer in the world. For example, 'Tidy up your room and I'll take you out and buy you a new pair of jeans this afternoon' (conditional positive) or 'Do that once more and you're grounded for a week' (conditional negative).

Each individual has one or more *target positive and target negative strokes*, respectively the things we like most and the things we like least about ourselves. When we are given our positive target stroke(s) we feel great pleasure; when we are given our target negative stroke(s) we feel great pain. As is the case of each person's more general propensity to invite positive or negative strokes, target strokes, too, are usually conditioned in childhood. Some common positive target strokes are for looks, intelligence, generosity, and sympathy; some common negative target strokes are for stupidity, selfishness, meanness, and untrustworthiness.

A particular person's target strokes can be ascertained by

direct questioning, such as, 'What attributes others describe you as having make you feel particularly good/bad about yourself?', but a clue to them is what kind of strokes the person tends to give to others. Thus, 'What a kind woman' is likely to be said by a woman whose own (positive) target stroke is kindness; 'What a mean bastard' is likely to be said by someone whose own (negative) target stroke is meanness.

We tend to assume that other people's target strokes are the same as our own, but in this we are often mistaken. Finding out what somebody's target strokes are, and often giving them their target positive stroke, and scrupulously avoiding giving them their target negative stroke (despite their provocation), is greatly conducive to increasing the sum total of happiness in the world. Easier said than done! Many unhappy relationships revolve around each person continually giving the other their negative target strokes.

Making Sense of the World

Why do we go on seeking the same strokes over and over again? Why, for example, does a woman who has been told from infancy that she has gorgeous blue eyes go on wanting this stroke over and over again, in preference to some new strokes that she has not received before? She does so because her 'gorgeous blue eyes' are a significant part of the sense she makes of herself in relation to other people and the world.

When we are newborn and entering a world which – we infer from the behaviour of newborn babies – is an utterly chaotic, undifferentiated blob of experience, our brains are hard-wired for us to acquire knowledge about the world, both physical and psychological, as quickly as we possibly can, to enable us, step by step, to achieve independence and autonomy, and not have to be looked after by other people in order to survive.

In the acquisition of our knowledge of objective, physical reality, we are all very much alike. We differ from each other to the extent that we each have our own particular ways of perceiving that highlight some, and gloss over other, aspects of reality. Thus an artist may tend to see 'nothing but' colours and shapes, a banker will focus on the economic aspects of reality, and a naturalist may find city streets 'empty'. Nevertheless, allowing for the differences of focus that are conditioned by differences of interest, by and large, we have all been taught to interpret the world in ways that all sane people call 'correct'. Experientially, we probably learn nearly all the basic laws of physics by the time we are one year of age: hot and cold, rough and smooth, heavy and light ... which get reinforced and elaborated through the answers our parents and others give to our multitudinous questions in the first few years of our lives.

Consider, for example, a conversation between a three-year-old and his or her mother.

Three-year-old: Mummy, why won't my ball stay up?

Mother: Because everything falls back to the ground.

Three-year-old: Why?

Mother: Gravity makes everything fall down.

And if this three-year-old asks her nursery school teacher the same question, she will almost certainly be given more or less the same answer.

Thus, we share with all sane others a collection of *conventions we agree on concerning how to perceive and understand physical reality.* This was brought home to me by one of my daughters when she was about four and she asked me, 'Mummy, why is it that all the big aeroplanes are at the airport and all the little ones in the sky?' And I, of course, (in the name of sanity), replied, 'Well actually the ones in the sky are really big too. They just look little because they are a long way away.' But, in giving this reply, I realized with some poignancy that, in teaching children about the nature of reality, we are *closing their minds.* There is no *metaphysical reason* why I could not have replied to my daughter, 'Well actually the ones at the airport are really little too. They just look big because they are very close.' No doubt we could construct a completely self-consistent theory of physical reality in which we would agree that things only *look* big when they are close, and are *really* small; but we have decided to put it the other way round.

Each answer a child gets to his questions about physical reality makes the world a more *predictable* place. He now *knows* a bit more and feels that much more *secure*.

Who has not, at some time, found gratification in *testing the security of our knowledge* about the world by actions, for example, like covering a burning candle with a glass and 'proving' – again – that, yes, fire does need a continuous supply of oxygen to go on burning?

There are thousands of actual stimuli bombarding our brains at every moment of our waking lives, yet our brains are only capable of processing a handful of them at a time. So we are programmed to exclude as 'white noise' the vast majority of stimuli, in favour of attending only to the very small number that we need to be aware of to survive and be effective in our particular environment. Those unfortunate people who, by dint of innate brain damage or circumstantial experience, are incapable of blocking out the 'noise' of the world in favour of *highly selective perception*, are deemed insane.

And in exactly the same way, and in order to fulfil the same basic need to make sense of the world, so as to feel *secure* in it, we learn about psychological reality. Learning about physical reality enables us safely and confidently to interact with *things*; learning about psychological reality enables us safely and confidently to interact with *people*. Making sense of people means learning *how to give and get strokes*.

So, all the time we are asking our mothers and fathers about gravity and temperature, animals and birds, night and day, sand and snow ... we are also asking about life and death, love and hate, anger, jealousy, ownership rights and sharing, happiness and unhappiness, good and bad, reward and punishment, etc. etc. And by the time we first leave home to go to school, we are basically equipped to get our stroke needs met in the world at large.

However, we all make one huge mistake – a mistake that most people continue to make for the rest of their lives. *We presume that just because everybody else's physical reality is the same as our own, so everybody else's psychological reality is also the same as our own. It isn't.*

True, there are areas of overlap between one person's and another's psychological realities, or else we would all continually fail to get strokes from other people. But what we witnessed and were told about people in our early family life may be very different from what our best friend witnessed and was told about in her family. Some families are generally amiable, some sad, some angry and quarrelsome, some loving, some rejecting, some quiet, some noisy, some organized, some chaotic, some changeable. But it is on the basis of the characteristics of our own particular family that *each of us decides what human nature and our psychological world will be about.*

In this way one child becomes the man whose greatest happiness is his close and loving family life, his greatest difficulty in life being his constant worry about money. Another becomes renowned in his field of work, and feels immensely rewarded by the honours heaped on him, but constantly does battle with his inclination to alcoholism. One woman is constantly appreciated for her femininity and beauty but feels inferior for never having completed her secondary schooling, while another is profoundly positively stroked as a mother but miserable as a wife.

Thus – for the good and the bad in our lives – what is *relevant* to one person is *irrelevant* to, and therefore not 'heard' by another.

The differences between people's target negative strokes was made vivid to me some years ago, a few days before Christmas, when I was about to conduct a group therapy session. The group was already assembled and, as I walked into the room, I heard one group member saying to another, with obvious discomfort, 'Thank you very much for your Christmas card. Um, um, we're not sending any this year, but I hope you don't think we're ungrateful,' and I suddenly realized that she was giving herself her own target negative stroke – ingratitude – which provided me with a wonderful opportunity to demonstrate the variability of people's target negative strokes. That situation, bumping into somebody who has sent you a Christmas card, when it's too late for you to send them one - no big deal, but we've all experienced it and been inclined to have some, however mild, uncomfortable feeling.

So I took advantage of this situation, which we have all known, and said, 'OK everybody, it's December the 21st and you bump into somebody who has sent you a Christmas card, and you haven't sent them one. Quickly and spontaneously tell us how you feel.' We got 'guilty', 'embarrassed', 'angry', 'ungrateful', 'ashamed', 'worried', and 'selfish', but what was most fascinating was the looks of amazed disbelief on people's faces, as others declared their target strokes, as if to say, 'That's not the feeling you're supposed to have.' There was silence at the end, and then, finally, one of the 'guilty' ones turned to the 'ungrateful' one and said, 'But you do feel guilty *for* being ungrateful, don't you?' And the 'ungrateful' one said, 'No, I don't.'

Different strokes for different folks!

With respect to our knowledge and expectations of the physical world we are all pretty much alike, with some variation; with respect to our knowledge and expectations of the psychological world we are very different from each other, with some overlap. The security that comes from *predictability* makes us all seek the same strokes over and over again.

Chapter Two

Foraging for Strokes

The Inefficacy of Punishment

Strokes are given people for their *intrinsic attributes*, such as for their 'gorgeous blue eyes'; and they are also given for *behaviour*, something they have done. When a stroke is given for behaviour, for example, a child being stroked by his mother for looking after his little brother so well while she was out, not only does that stroke make the child feel good about himself, but it will also make him even more inclined in future to look after his brother well, when he is next asked to.

All strokes, positive and negative, that are given for behaviour, increase the probability of that behaviour occurring in the future. Positive strokes make us feel good about ourselves, and make the behaviour we are stroked for more likely in future; negative strokes make us feel bad about ourselves, *and* make the behaviour more likely in future. *Punishment is negative strokes,* and negative strokes, every bit as much as positive strokes, increase the likelihood of the behaviour they were given for being repeated in future.

Why is this understanding, that punishment (negative strokes) doesn't work, so anti-commonsense? It is anti-common-sense because, for the moment that the punishment is being inflicted, the behaviour that it is being given for diminishes to zero. But the moment the punishment is lifted, the behaviour not only goes back to its original level, but goes higher, at least until its average expression is returned to the level it was at before the punishment was inflicted. So if you have a rat in a cage doing something or other it has been trained to do at a certain frequency, and the experimenter gives it an electric shock, it immediately stops doing it for as long as the electric shock is being inflicted, but when the shock is lifted – Wow!

The person who was responsible for teaching us the inefficacy of punishment was the behavioural psychologist, B. F. Skinner, by whose 'schedules of reinforcement' (that is stroke schedules) he taught pigeons to play ping pong! He did this through systematically 'shaping' their behaviour, by rewarding (giving positive strokes to) the pigeons with a pellet of food every time they arbitrarily moved their beaks in the right direction for picking up the (miniature) bat, banging the ball with the bat ... etc., until – believe it or not – he had them playing ping –pong. In systematically training his pigeons, Skinner theoretically proved the inefficacy of punishment, and the efficacy of rewards, but this knowledge has always been known instinctively by animal trainers. It is only in the 'training' of each other that human beings are stupid enough to believe that punishment can be effective in eliminating undesirable behaviour or promoting desired behaviour. In prisons and schools, the same people are given the same punishments over and over again. Just as is the case for pigeons, the punishment of human beings 'works' only for the brief period that the punishment is actually being inflicted. *The only way that undesirable behaviour can be eliminated is by ignoring it, that is, giving it no strokes at all* (admittedly not easy).

Stroke Schedules

The understanding that Skinner has also given us is awareness of the different powers of different *schedules of reinforcement* (strokes). There are three different schedules in which strokes can be given, if your intention is to teach or train somebody in some knowledge or skill: a *ratio schedule* in which every 'nth' (e.g. fifth, tenth) appropriate response is rewarded; an *interval schedule* in which rewards are given after a certain interval of time (e.g. every four minutes); and an *intermittent schedule* in which rewards are given in terms of both ratio and interval schedules, and are thereby unpredictable to the person or animal being trained. *Intermittent reinforcement is overwhelmingly the most powerful training schedule there is.* (Hence my propensity to addiction in playing solitaire on my computer!)

This brings up another anti-commonsense truth. Parents often unwittingly give their children's undesirable behaviour intermittent reinforcement, with positive as well as negative strokes. Consider the mother of a two-year-old who is having a temper-tamper because he wants a chocolate biscuit, and Mummy has said no. He is stamping his foot and screaming, and Mummy grits her teeth and keeps on saying no until, after about five minutes, she can stand it no longer, so she gives him the chocolate biscuit he is demanding.

The next day – or the next time – the child starts screaming for a chocolate biscuit that Mummy has said no to, his mother might, commonsensically, say to herself, I'm going to hang on this time, and she manages to bear the screaming for ten minutes before she gives in. After the first five minutes, the child's screams get louder. After all, it only took five minutes screaming to get that biscuit yesterday, so what's wrong? Perhaps she can't hear me, so I'd better raise my pitch. His mother, on the other hand, might (mistakenly) congratulate herself that she at least hung on for longer this time; but what she has actually done is create the most powerful learning in the child to *go on screaming, when he wants something.* What is going on in the child's head, (though he probably can't articulate it verbally, even to himself,) is, 'Oh well, the first time it took five minutes, but today she took ten minutes, so now I know it's worth screaming for ten minutes.' The next day, if Mummy is stupid enough to go on with this schedule, thinking she is gaining something, the screaming gets louder and more prolonged...

The moral of the story is that if you ever want to stop anybody doing what you don't want them to do, there is only one way to achieve your goal, and that is to give the behaviour no strokes at all. As I have already admitted, this is much easier said than done. So if you want to eliminate some habitual behaviour in another, and you don't think you have the strength yet, confidently to *never* stroke the behaviour again, then give it a stroke – positive or negative – for the behaviour, *immediately*. Then, when the time comes that you are confident enough of your own strength of will to *never* stroke the behaviour again, the other person will know very quickly that the behaviour is not going to be stroked any more, and they will give up. (But do remember that in any relationship, when one party ceases giving strokes to some habitual behaviour in the other, that other is bound, at first, to escalate their provocative behaviour, wondering what is wrong with the one who is no longer responding predictably. So when you decide to stop – now and forever – giving strokes for some behaviour in another, make sure you know you have the strength, and are prepared to resist an even higher level of provocative behaviour than previously.)

Six Stroke Diets

Transactional Analysis observes that our ways of being in the world reflect the variable *value and healthfulness* of strokes we give and receive in everyday life, just as there is variable calorific value and healthfulness in the food and drink we consume. Some people graze on food and drink throughout the day, some people like one big meal a day and very little else, and other people are somewhere in between. Whether we are grazers or prefer one big meal a day, we are similarly different from each other in our preferences for lots of little strokes or a few big ones to meet our daily calorific needs.

The foods and the strokes that we were given when we were young children become our favourite foods and our favourite strokes. It is very difficult to dissuade people from unhealthy foods they have become habituated to, as Jamie Oliver has discovered; and it is similarly difficult to wean people off their habituation to negative strokes (although a lot of psychotherapy is about attempting this).

There are six different *stroke diets*: Withdrawal, Rituals, Pastimes, Work (and personal hobbies), Games, and Intimacy.

From Withdrawal to Intimacy, the (calorific) value of strokes given and received increases, *but so, too, does vulnerability.* Generally, each of us chooses our own optimum balance between stroke value and vulnerability, using all of the available ways, in mixed proportions, to fill our stroke hunger.

In the limiting case of Withdrawal, we absent ourselves from all company, and neither give nor receive any positive or negative strokes, and so are completely invulnerable to others.

The other limiting case is Intimacy, in which we experience totally open, spontaneous psychological nakedness in relation to another person, and which contains the highest value strokes on offer in the world. They are the wonderfully biggest strokes, including all the 'I love yous' we get. But Intimacy is also the relationship to another in which we are most excruciatingly vulnerable to the other person's responses to us, and to the fear of rejection by that other.

In between, there are Rituals, Pastimes, Work, and Games From Withdrawal to Intimacy the stroke yield increases, but so too does our vulnerability. So everybody, by dint of a combination of innate temperament and conditioning, chooses by what proportions of each of the six options they prefer to get their daily stroke needs met.

Rituals are extremely predictable ways in which human beings interact with each other. We get Ritual strokes at cocktail parties, weddings, funerals, saying good morning to a passing acquaintance, religious observances, casual conversations with people in shops and at bus stops, with birthday cakes and candles, Christmas dinners, etc., whereby we get predictable strokes that enable us to feel secure in our relationship to society and to our families. Ritual strokes don't have much individual value, but they are a very important, virtually fail-safe way of getting at least some strokes, and they are particularly relied on by lonely people.

Pastimes are somewhat more selective than Rituals. We Pastime with people whom we may know very little about except the interests we share with them, whether it be playing Scrabble, bridge, tennis, squash, 'girls nights out' (where the talk is typically of clothes, children, and men), 'boys nights out' (where the talk is typically of cars and football and women) ...etc. In Pastiming, we are a bit more vulnerable than when we are engaging in Rituals, but the stroke –value is proportionally higher.

Work is a very rich source of strokes for most people, providing much significant giving and getting of strokes from and to bosses and subordinates and in peer group interactions. And, of course, it entails considerable vulnerability to others, including such risks as being demoted or made redundant as well as the possibility of praise and promotion. Work also enables us to get quasi-strokes from ourselves through the satisfaction we get for a job well done. The great stroke value we get from the interactions we have with others in our daily work (which includes, of course, some Ritual and Pastiming strokes) makes it difficult for some people to get enough strokes from being self-employed, even though they may otherwise wish to be.

Games

Because Intimacy is such an utterly naked situation and is therefore so overwhelmingly fraught with vulnerability, and the pain of rejection in an intimate relationship can feel unbearable, many people forever shy away from true Intimacy. What they choose instead is Games – the psychological games we all play sometimes – discovered by Eric Berne and made famous in his book, *Games People Play*. Apart from true (and rare) Intimacy, Games are the source of the greatest number of highly valued strokes that most people seek and get, even though all Games end with some kind of negative feeling (usually involving our target negative strokes).

A Game is a *set series of ulterior interactions between people, ending in a negative stroke for all players.* Each protagonist has a hidden agenda, an aim to gain psychological advantage over the other, while insisting on the propriety of his or her own motives. Although there is an unconscious component in Game-playing, there is also, in most people when they embark on a Game, some knowledge of 'Here I go again.' We are all exiles from paradise; we all play Games sometimes.

Eric Berne delineated a few dozen different Games, and analyzed out the moves that each party makes in the course of the Game, and the painful payoff (negative stroke) that each player inevitably experiences at the end. And many other Transactional Analysis practitioners added to the list of analyzed Games until, by the mid-1970s, the number of named Games was becoming unwieldy, a situation which was overcome by a man called Steven Karpman, who generalized all the particularities of different Games into the Drama Triangle, involving the *roles* of Persecutor, Rescuer, and Victim.

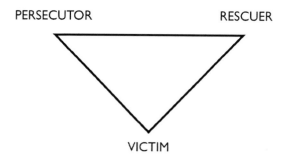

Figure 2.1 The Drama Triangle

The Persecutor role deludes itself into seeing itself as *righteous;* the Rescuer role deludes itself into seeing itself as *selfless;* and the Victim role deludes itself into seeing itself as *helpless.* When we play Games, we move around amongst these roles, starting out in one role and moving around the triangle in the course of the Game, but each player ending up in the role which is congruent with his or her own favourite bad feeling. We choose to play Games with others whose 'hand' in the Game is complementary to our own; and we can pick somebody who will play the hand complementary to our own from a hundred yards away, with unerring accuracy and precision.

Although there are umpteen different Games and umpteen different Payoffs, Payoffs can be generalized as either of the form 'I am Kicked' or 'Now I've Got You, You Son-of-a-Bitch'. The former Payoff is usually reached by people likely to have felt in childhood – for whatever reason – that they needed to *earn* their parents' love, and perhaps to 'make Mummy or Daddy better'; the latter Payoff is usually reached by people whose pains in childhood have prompted them to seek *revenge* on their parents, by using other people as 'bastard' substitutes for them.

Probably the most played Game in the world is 'Why Don't You? Yes, But...', and it exemplifies well how the Drama Triangle works. A young woman (Victim) phones her friend (Rescuer), saying, 'It's terrible, my landlady's selling her house and she's given me notice to quit my room at the end of the month, and I don't know what to do.' Her Rescuer friend replies, 'Well why don't you get hold of the early edition of the Evening Standard, it has a good selection of rooms to let,' to which Victim says, 'Yes, but I can't get off work in the morning, and by lunchtime everything's gone.' Rescuer comes up with several other suggestions, to all of which Victim responds, 'Yes, but ...' Eventually, Rescuer gets irritated, switches into Persecutor and says, 'Look, don't waste your time and mine. If everything I suggest is no use to you, don't ask me.' Victim then switches into Persecutor and says,

'I always knew you weren't a real friend,' and slams the phone down, giving herself a 'Now I've Got You, You Son-of-a-Bitch, and ' Nobody ever gives me what I want' payoff, and leaving the other in Victim, with her Kicked payoff , 'No matter how much I do for people, they never appreciate me.' A very simple and very widely played Game throughout the world!

So if Games inevitably end up with bad feelings for both parties, why do we play them? We play them, even though we know they are going to end painfully, because there are lots and lots of strokes given and received along the way. The melodrama is highly stroke calorific. It might be junk food, which gives us a stomach ache, but we know exactly how much pain we will get, and the pleasure in the feeding is 'worth it'. Games feel 'safe', because they are almost as predictable as Rituals, and the pain they bring us is safely circumscribed. For many people, 'intimacy' is the name they give to the Games they play.

Chapter Three

Ego States and Transactions

Ego States in General

Eric Berne arrived at his concept of the ego states through his practice as a psychoanalytically-oriented psychiatrist. One day, one of his patients arrived at his office, and Eric Berne greeted him with, 'How are you?' to which the man replied, 'Are you talking to the big shot lawyer or the little boy?' which illuminates the fact that our egos – the conscious part of ourselves – is not one entity. Indeed, as Eric Berne discerned, there are *three distinct components that make up the totality of our conscious 'selves'*, which he named our Parent, Adult, and Child ego states.

The corollary of this fact is that *we are all, by definition, inconsistent,* because these three parts of us as likely as not to disagree with each other over many matters; and I have seen this fact alone give immediate relief to many people who previously felt it somehow 'wrong' to be inconsistent, that inconsistency required an apology.

Our three ego states are genuine existential states of being, amongst which we voluntarily move, hour by hour, minute by minute, second by second, throughout our waking lives. (In this respect, they are unlike the *roles* of Persecutor, Rescuer, and Victim, which are actually contained in an inauthentic, conditioned part of the Child ego state (which will be elucidated in Chapter 5). Changing ego states is like changing gear.

The three ego states are always drawn as in Figure 3.1, three touching but not overlapping circles, and their names are always capitalized to distinguish them from our ordinary usage of those words.

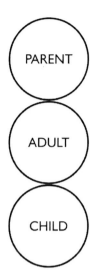

Figure 3.1. The Ego States

Each ego state has its contents and its functions.

Our Parent ego state contains our values, beliefs, moral code, and generalizations about life; its function is to protect and control ourselves and others.

Our Adult ego state contains our knowledge and skills; its function is to process, evaluate, and store information and skills in an objective way; it can be conveniently thought of as our computer.

Our Child ego state contains all our feelings, innate and conditioned; its function is simply to express itself.

The table below should enable you readily to grasp the essential contents and forms of expression of each of the ego states.

Characteristics of the Ego States

	Parent	Adult	Child
Words	good/bad,	how, what, why	wow, want, can't, won't,
	should/	when, where,	wish, hope,
	shouldn't,	who, interesting,	please, thank you, I wonder,
	must/mustn't,	practical,	I have a feeling that...
	always/never, right/wrong	That's phoney!	
Voice	concerned	even, calm	energetic, free, loud,
	comforting,		whining, excited, pleading
	critical		
Gestures	open arms,	thoughtful,	uninhibited, loose,
or expression/	points finger,	alert, open	spontaneous, naive,
	frowns, smiles		cute, sad, happy, assertive, whimsical, knowing
Attitude	judgemental,	erect,	curious, compliant,
	understanding, caring, giving, authoritarian,	evaluative of facts	defiant, ashamed, volatile, creative, fun-loving, manipulative,
	moralistic		hypothesizing

The totality of our Parent ego state is our *character*, which is essentially formed by the explicit exhortations of our parents and teachers.

The totality of our Adult is our *knowledge and skills*.

The totality of our Child is our *personality*, which is the combination of our innate *temperament*, combined with our *conditioned* ways of responding emotionally to other people and the world.

Other species have Child and Adult ego states, but it is only human beings who have a Parent ego state. (Other species behave in parental ways, but this is pre-programmed behaviour, a part of their Child ego state, called the Adapted Child, which will be elaborated in Chapter 5). It is our Parent ego state which enables us, as human beings, to talk about 'right and wrong', 'good and bad', the meaning of life, whether or not God exists, how we should behave and be, such as to be kind, generous, honest and truthful, and to work hard. These concepts require a well-tenanted Parent ego state, the absence of which, in extremis, results in what we call a sociopathic character disorder.

We are *in* one or other of our ego states at any given moment. None of them is 'better' or 'worse' than the others. We need all of them to function well in everyday life, although people are different from each other in the relative amounts of energy they have in each ego state. Some people have such noticeably different proportions of Parent, Adult and Child in their make-up that we recognize them as distinct types.

Parent-type people tend to put their moral principles above all else, and look at life in terms of 'right versus wrong' and 'good versus bad'. They are honest, kind, reliable, solid citizens. Other people tend to respond to them with compliance and respect or angry rebelliousness.

Adult-type people tend to value most highly their own and other people's rationality. They are clear-headed, practical, and knowledgeable. Other people tend to seek them out for some specific purpose, such as their professional knowledge.

Child-type people are basically emotional, and respond to life impulsively. They tend to be excitable, charming, and fun-loving, but quite inconsiderate of other people's wishes and needs.

A completely balanced person has his energy evenly distributed between his three ego states, as in Figure 3.1, but such perfect balance is rare. And it would be a pretty dull world if we all were so balanced. We need people with a little extra Parent to be our good doctors and nurses and counsellors and ministers of religion. We need people with a little extra Adult to be our good lawyers and computer programmers and accountants. And we need people with a little extra Child to be our artists and entertainers, inventors and dress designers.

Figure 3.2 represents the six possible ways in which energy may be unevenly distributed amongst the ego states of a person. (For the sake of completion, the perfectionist reader may like to add the instances of two ego states having equal amounts of energy, and the third more or less.)

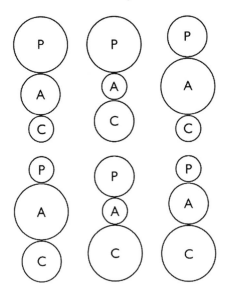

Figure 3.2 Which Are You?

Functional health can be defined as having *enough energy* in each ego state to be able to go *into* the one appropriate to the situation we find ourselves in. So, for example, it is appropriate to be in our Parent if we are signing a petition on behalf of a cause we believe in; it is appropriate to be in our Adult when we are writing a cheque to pay a bill; and it is appropriate to be in our Child when riding a rollercoaster or being at a party. If we are in an inappropriate ego state, we are unlikely to be comfortable and/or to be effective in our responses, and other people are unlikely to like being with us.

In any kind of difficult situation, when in doubt, the safest place to be is in our Adult; in it, we may not do much good, but neither do we do any harm; and going into our Adult can help us avoid having bad Child feelings of our own in response to another's rudeness or bad behaviour.

To help you consolidate your understanding of the Adult and Parent ego states, here is some further description of each of them. (The Child ego state is simply our feelings and their expression, although we will see in Chapter 5 that its structure contains some complexity.)

The Parent Ego State

When we are very young, mostly in the period between three and six years of age, we are *taught* by our parents to be honest, kind, truthful, helpful, and generally to share with and care for other people. By the age of about six, we *believe in* all these moral principles, and these principles constitute our *character*, which is our Parent ego state.

As well as reflecting what each of our particular parents taught us, our Parent also reflects values that operate in society as a whole. In fact, there are probably a few Parent values that are common to all societies everywhere, such as that murder is wrong, as is sex between parents and their children or between brothers and sisters. In our particular society, kindness, tolerance, achievement, honesty, truthfulness, reliability, generosity, and good manners are examples of positive Parent values that most people are taught; and violence, brutality, meanness, dishonesty, laziness, and bad manners are generally considered by most people's Parents to be negative character traits.

Each family, as well as having values that are shared by most people in the society of which the family is a part, usually have particular values of their own, often handed down from generation to generation. Some families, for example, are very keen on educational attainment, some value financial success, some value of being of service to the community. Some families are religious, some intellectual, and some place great value on family life.

What does your Parent contain? That is, what do you *believe in*? Begin by listing the beliefs and values you have that are common to most people in our society, then add those that you were taught in your particular family. One way to pinpoint your Parent values is by completing the sentence, 'The most important things to remember in life are ...' Some of these will be about what you should *be*, others about what you should *do*.

The Adult Ego State

Our Adult grows most naturally and easily between the ages of eighteen months and three years, being especially associated with our learning to talk; and again from about six to twelve years of age.

Our Adult contains all the basic knowledge and skills that everybody needs to manage well, in a practical way, in the grown-up world, as well as extra knowledge and interests that each person develops for him - or herself. It is our Adult that asks Why and What and When and How and Where and Who. And it is with our Adult that we learn how to blow our noses, build a tower of blocks, use the toilet, wash and dry our hands, draw a picture, dress ourselves and tie our shoelaces, feed ourselves, make a sandcastle with a bucket and spade, do a jigsaw puzzle. *Our Adult provides us with ways of finding strokes from the inanimate world as well as from people.*

It is our Adult that knows the trick of peeling onions without crying, that can touch type, and knows enough French to get by on a holiday in France. It is our Adult that budgets our income and expenditure, writes shopping lists, reads car manuals and recipes and instructions for filling in a form. The more Adult skills and interests we have, the less dependent we are on other people to provide us with all the strokes we need. What solitary activities does your Adult enable you to enjoy?

As well as all the solitary pleasures our Adult offers us, it also contributes greatly to the pleasures we derive from being with other people. Think of all the ways of enjoying being with other people that depend on your having appropriate Adult knowledge and skills – tennis, football, cricket, squash, scrabble, chess, bridge, and all the conversations you have with people who have similar jobs or interests to yourself. What activities with other people does your Adult enable you to enjoy?

Transactions in General

Since each person has three ego states, any two people, between them, have six ego states. And when two people meet, whether or not they say anything to each other, as long as they make eye contact or touch each other in any way, they are engaged in *transactions* with each other (which is just another way of saying giving and getting strokes). As you can see from Figure 3.3, one person beginning to transact with another can choose (consciously or semi-consciously) to be in any of his or her three ego states and to address any of the three ego states of the other person. So we have nine different choices concerning the quality of the beginning transaction we initiate with another person.

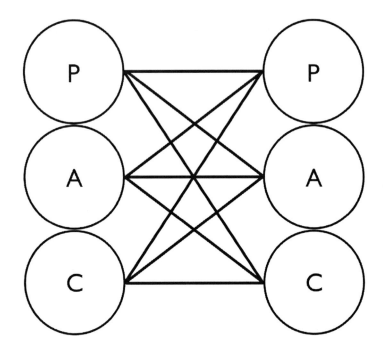

Figure 3.3. Two People, Six Ego States, Nine Ways of Transacting

It is common knowledge that about 55 per cent of the meaning of any communication between two people is contained in visual stimuli, another 38 per cent in auditory stimuli, including tone of voice, accent, inflexion and volume, and only about 7 per cent in the objective meaning of the words uttered. So, with only the stimulus of printed words on a page, it is difficult to define the nature of a transaction unambiguously. Nevertheless, for the purposes of demonstration, let us assume that the essential meaning is contained in the actual words spoken, and look at an example of each of the nine ways that one person can initiate a transaction with another, even though, in principle, each statement could be said in each of the nine ways. Try saying, 'What's for supper?' in each of the nine possible ways!

1   Stranger to stranger in the street: Excuse me, could you tell

me the time? (Adult to Adult)

2 Boy to girl: You're the most beautiful girl I've ever met. (Child to Child)

3 Husband to wife: Shall we take the kids out for a treat this weekend? (Parent to Parent)

4 Pupil to teacher: What should I do next? (Adult to Parent)

5 Ten-year-old to his parents: You stay in bed, and I'll make breakfast. (Parent to Child)

6 Mother to whining three-year-old on the bus: We'll soon be home and then you can have some lunch and a nice rest. (Adult to Child)

7 Father to son: You'll never saw a straight piece of wood that way. Here, let me show you how. (Parent to Adult)

8 Girl to boy: You *are* clever! (Child to Adult)

9 Woman to man: Will you buy me a diamond engagement ring? (Child to Parent)

In practice, the majority of transactions between people are Adult to Adult, Parent to Parent, Child to Child, Child to Parent, and Parent to Child. Transactions between one person's Adult and another's Parent usually take place between teachers and pupils, and transactions between one person's Adult and another's Child usually take place between a grown-up and an emotionally aroused child. But always remember that all children over the age of about six have a Parent ego state, and all grown-ups have a Child ego state. And there are inevitably some transactions that have fuzzy edges, as it were, so we may not always be able to define precisely and unambiguously which ego state in one person is transacting with which ego state in another, although most often the diagnosis is simple and unequivocal.

Complementary Transactions

Now let's consider some pairs of transactions. For example, a husband arrives home from work, with a streaming cold. How might his wife begin to transact with him? She might say, from her Parent to his Child, 'You poor thing, you look full of cold. Get into bed, and I'll make you a nice hot toddy.' (Stimulus of Figure 3.4) Or she might say, from her Adult to his Adult, 'You look full of cold. There's some Vitamin C and aspirin in the bathroom cupboard if you want them.' (Stimulus of Figure 3.5). Or she might say, from her Child to his Child, 'Wow, you've got a corker. Keep away from me, I don't want it!' Or she might say, from her Child to his Parent, 'I hope you're not going to go on about this cold. Remember you promised to take me out tonight.'

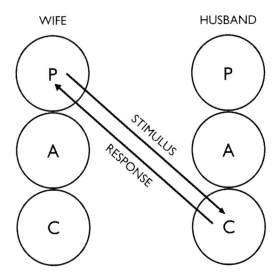

Figure 3.4 A complementary transaction

What might the husband's response be? To his wife's Parent to Child stimulus, 'Get into bed, and I'll make you a nice hot toddy,' he might respond, Child to Parent, 'Thank you, darling, that's just what I feel like.' (Figure 3.4). Or, in response to his wife's stimulus, 'Remember you promised to take me out tonight,' he might respond, Parent to Child, 'Well I'm sorry, but I'm going to have to break my promise.' In both of these examples, stimulus and response together form a *complementary transaction*. That is, the ego state that was addressed responded to the ego state that addressed it, so the communication (irrespective of the feelings involved) is clear and unambiguous.

Crossed Transactions

Of course, not all transactions are complementary. Consider, for example, in response to his wife's Adult to Adult stimulus, 'There's some aspirin and vitamin C in the bathroom cabinet,' the husband replies, 'Oh for goodness sake, don't you realize that once you've got a cold, there's nothing you can do about it,' (Figure 9a) you can quite clearly see that the lines are crossed. And that particular transaction, where an Adult to Adult stimulus gets a Parent to Child put-down or a Child to Parent stop-bossing-me-about response, is probably responsible for all the quarrels and all the wars that ever occur in the world.

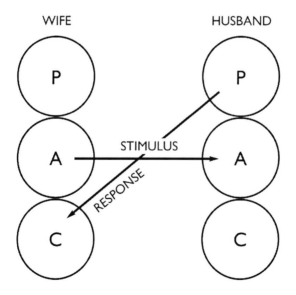

Figure 3.5 A crossed transaction

There are other kinds of crossed transactions though. Any transaction which is not one in which the ego state that was addressed replies to the ego state that addressed it is technically a crossed transaction. For example, if, in response to his wife's Adult to Adult, 'There's some aspirin and vitamin C in the bathroom cabinet,' he responds, Parent to Parent, 'We must get a kid-proof lock on this bathroom cabinet' (Figure 3.6), this is a crossed transaction, even though the lines of communication are diagrammatically parallel; he is not responding directly to what she said. Whether or not the outcome of a crossed transaction is happy, is another matter, just as it is in the case of complementary transactions, but in crossed transactions communication is handicapped by being unclear.

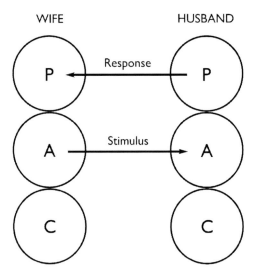

Figure 3.6 Another crossed transaction

Then there is another kind of crossed transaction, called an *angular crossed transaction*. Consider the case of the husband responding to his wife's Parent to Child, 'Get into bed, and I'll make you a nice hot toddy,' with a Child to Child, 'If you come with me.' (Figure 3.7). This is an angular crossed transaction because the ego state that was addressed responds, but to a different ego state from the one that addressed it.

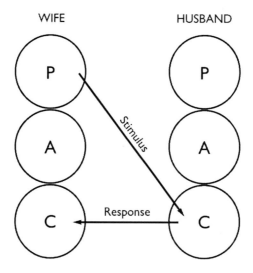

Figure 3.7 An angular crossed transaction

Duplex Transactions

But the majority of the transactions we have in our personal lives are more complex and contain *covert*, or hidden, messages. These are *duplex transactions*, in which communication *nominally* takes place between two ego states – usually, but not exclusively, Adult to Adult – but the real meaning of the transaction is unspoken – usually, but not exclusively, Child to Child. The covert part of the transaction, diagrammed by the dotted lines in Figure 3.8, is always the true communication.

An archetypal example of a covert transaction is in the sexual arena. For example, a man takes a woman out for the evening, then drives her home, and when they get to her place she says, 'Would you like to come in for a drink?' (Adult to Adult). Of course we – and they – know that the real transaction is 'Let's have sex at my place' (Child to Child), to which the undisguised response is, 'Yeah, let's' or 'No, I don't fancy you.' (Child to Child)

Such duplex transactions are a very important part of

MAN   WOMAN

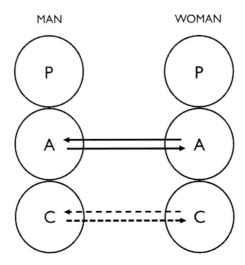

Figure 3.8 A Duplex Transaction

civilized behaviour, especially in the sexual area of our lives, where we are all most vulnerable. To this extent, they are designed to enable us to save face as we tentatively reach out to other people, sounding out and testing the ground, especially in new relationships. In the example I have given, he is most likely to respond to her covert invitation, with a covert message of his own, such as, 'Yes, I'm really quite thirsty.' On the other hand, if he responds, 'I'd love to, but I'd better get home, I've got an early start tomorrow,' his message is clear, but she is saved the humiliation of a direct rejection. Furthermore, were the man crude enough to reply to her covert invitation with, 'No I don't want sex with you,' she could 'legitimately' reply, Adult to Adult, 'I was only inviting you for a drink.'

The only trouble with covert transactions is that they are also involved in all Games, and it is a tightrope act for all of us to use covert duplex transactions in the name of civilization and good manners rather than in playing Games. Of course, some people will play Games around the authentically well-intentioned duplex transactions of another, which is a risk we take. Some covert communication is involved in virtually all of our social and intimate encounters.

There is also an angular type of duplex transaction, which I think is largely limited to the communication between sales people and their customers. Consider a middle-aged man in a clothing shop, trying on a suit, and the salesman saying, overtly Adult to Adult, 'It's a beautiful fit, sir, but perhaps you'd prefer something not so youthful looking.' The covert transaction here is the Adult to Child one, 'Buy this if you want to look younger.' (Figure 3.9) The salesman's aim is to 'hook' the customer's Child into the direct Child to

Adult response of 'I'll have it.' Should the customer see through the salesman's ploy, and be offended by it, he might, perhaps, go into his own Parent and say to the salesman's Child, 'I'll thank you to mind your manners,' to which the salesman could then 'legitimately' respond complementarily, from his Child to the customer's Parent, with 'Oh, I beg your pardon, sir. Did I say something wrong?'

(Is all this a Game or 'good salesmanship'? You be the judge.)

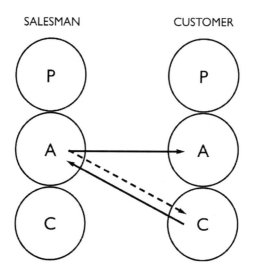

Figure 3.9 An angular duplex transaction

So covert transactions protect us and the other party from too much vulnerability, and it would be a horrible world if we had none, even though we have to be careful not to delude ourselves of our good intentions while actually setting up a get-nowhere, painful Game.

Chapter Four

The Whole Self in Action

Judgement, Compromise, and Creative Alternatives

Although we are *in* one or other of our ego states throughout our waking lives – and to some extent in our sleeping lives as well – and the measure of our functional health is whether we are in the appropriate ego state for our present circumstance, there are many choices and decisions we have to make in life that require the use of more than one ego state for a satisfactory outcome. For example, getting married, getting divorced, deciding whether or not to have children, taking out a mortgage, perhaps even choosing what car to buy – all require us to make up our minds with the support of more than one of our ego states. If we make such important choices and decisions with only one ego state, we are quite likely to be sorry afterwards, because the ego states we did not refer to may not approve the outcome. In relatively trivial matters, making consequential decisions on the basis of only one ego state's approval is often appropriate, but for the big decisions in life it is very important to refer to two or, ideally, all three ego states, with the aim of getting them to concur. This is not always easy.

A man called Arthur Rissman created a diagram, a triangle that describes how we do, in fact, use more than one ego state to make many choices and decisions, in small as well as in big matters. He called his diagram 'the trilog', which shows how the ego states collaborate with each other in pairs. Parent and Adult collaborate to form *judgements;* Parent and Child collaborate to form *compromises;* and Adult and Child collaborate to find *creative alternatives.*

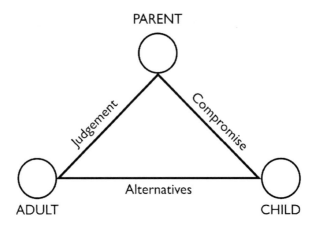

Figure 4.1 The trilog

Let's look at an example of each of these pairs.

Consider a magistrate in court who has before him a teenage lout, who has thrown a brick through a shop window. The boy is coming into court with his solicitor, and the solicitor says to the boy, 'You're lucky, we've got Judge Jones sitting today. You'll probably get off with a warning.' Or, the solicitor might say to the boy, 'Oh dear, we've got Judge Smith sitting today. We might be looking at a custodial sentence.' What is the difference between the two judges?

What the solicitor is referring to is his knowledge of the different qualities of the Parent ego states of those two magistrates, one of whom he knows to have a tender-hearted Parent that might say, 'Okay, boys will be boys. Off you go, but don't let me see you again.' Or the tough Parent magistrate might say, 'I have zero tolerance of this kind of behaviour. I'm making an example of you, and sending you down for six months.'

But when either magistrate passes sentence – whether lenient or harsh – he is not passing sentence solely with his Parent, but with a combination of his Parent and the (Adult) facts and reality of the law. The law will prescribe a certain range of penalties for particular crimes, and it is between the minimum and maximum penalties that the magistrate will bring to bear the values and beliefs of his Parent ego state.

And for all of us, in our everyday lives, there are occasions when we also have to make judgements, blending the (Adult) facts of the matter with our (Parent) beliefs and values. Ideally, the facts and our values will immediately concur, but often they don't. Consider, for example, a mother and father who have socialist Parent ego state values, and so believe in state education for their children. But the Adult facts are that the only state schools available for their children are very bad schools. Through dialogue, the *impasse* between their Parent and Adult will be resolved through one ego state giving way, at least partly, to the other, and they will thereby make a *judgement* leading to a decision. The uncomfortable feeling we have before our Parent and Adult have jointly come to a judgement is the *anxiety of indecisiveness*.

Now consider a teenage girl whose Child ego state has exhibitionistic impulses, and would like to display her body as a nightclub stripper. But as soon as her Child expresses that impulse to herself, she hears her Parent ego state (and perhaps her actual mother and father) come down on her with a very hefty thump, along the lines of 'Did we bring you up to be a prostitute? What a disgusting thing you want to do.' Because there is no Adult reality involved here, there is nothing factual to stop her from becoming a nightclub stripper; but if she does, a great deal of the pleasure her Child is looking for will be spoiled by the invocation of guilt or shame (or some other bad feeling) imposed on her by her Parent's wrath. So, healthily, instead of ignoring her Parent, and feeling sorry afterwards, she will have a dialogue between her Parent and Child. In response to her Parent's horror at the idea of her being a nightclub stripper, her Child might say to it, 'Well, all right then. What if I become an artist's model?' And her Parent might reply, 'Well I don't think that's a particularly nice profession, but all right, if you really want to.' So she goes ahead and becomes an artist's model, the matter having been resolved by a *compromise* in which her Child and her Parent each get some, but not all, of what they ideally want. The uncomfortable feeling we have before our Parent and Child have jointly arrived at a compromise is the *anxiety of conflict*. (The ability to compromise between our own Child and somebody else's Child or Parent, or between our own Parent and somebody else's Child or Parent is probably *the* mark of our having achieved the highest level of emotional literacy and maturity.)

Now consider a man whose Child yearns to live in a five-bedroom house on the edge of Hyde Park, but the Adult reality is that he hasn't got the money, and nor will anybody lend it to him, so he just can't have it. So what he healthily does is brainstorm, which is the dialogue between Adult and Child whereby the Child comes up with *alternatives* that might be possible within the constraints of the relevant (Adult) reality. For example, amongst the ideas his Child and Adult may consider are a one-bedroom flat on the edge of Hyde Park or a five-bedroom house in Swindon. Thus he finds realistic alternatives to his original, unattainable desire.

All dialogue of that kind between the Adult and the Child is creative, and all creative acts of any kind have the quality of Adult-Child dialogue. If you think of such acts in terms of an actual artist – a painter say – whose Child is, in principle, free to paint whatever picture it feels like, she is still going to have to create (chosen, Adult) constraints in order to paint the picture. She has to decide what size to make the picture, what shape, what colours to use, etc. Without such self-imposed constraints on her Child by her Adult, we would just have the daubing of a chimpanzee.

The creative process is not limited to those people who are actual creative artists or musicians or writers ... It occurs to all of us in our everyday lives. One instance of this, which has stayed in my memory, although it was a trivial matter, occurred when I was about ten years old. I was standing in the kitchen with my mother while she was making supper. The telephone rang, and it was my father, who said he was bringing somebody home with him for supper. My mother's face immediately dropped in horror, and she said, 'Oh goodness, we haven't got enough food.' Then I saw her face relax as she walked over to the sink, got two cups of water and poured them in the pan of soup on the stove. For some reason – presumably my appreciation of the creativity of her act – I thought that was wonderful. We all do things like this all the time.

Out of my understanding of the essential Adult-Child dialogue associated with creativity, I have formulated my own definition of creativity (or art), namely, that art is the outcome of the *struggle* to reconcile desire (Child) with reality (Adult).

The uncomfortable feeling we have before our Adult and Child have found satisfactory creative alternatives is the *anxiety of frustration or despair*.

So, in summary, we move from *indecisiveness to judgement*; from *conflict to compromise*; and from *despair or frustration to creative alternatives*.

In the most critically consequential situations in our lives, we really need all three ego states to endorse the choices we make. I believe this is why sport, team games in particular, have always been highly valued in educational theory, from the ancient Greeks to the present day, because they 'stroke up' and train all three ego states at the same time. So if you look at the middle of the trilog (Figure 4.1) and imagine 'the whole self' of a boy playing football being there, he is connected (by the dotted lines) to all three of his ego states: his Parent is obeying the rules of the game, his Adult is expressing and acquiring skills, and his Child is having a wonderful time!

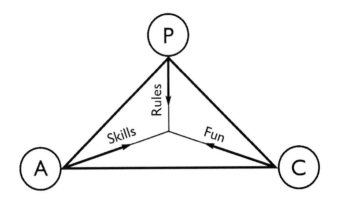

Figure 4.2 A boy playing football – the whole self in harmony

Prejudice, Confusion, and Delusion

Unfortunately, we are so constructed that our attempts to formulate judgements, compromises, and creative alternatives are sometimes thwarted by the ego states that are involved in the debate being equally energized, but opposed to each other, each being unwilling to give way to the other. They just keep bashing away at each other, chronically, and our experience is of preoccupation with the impasse, which uses up a lot of energy, and creates increasing anxiety in us. The energy deployed in the impasse is locked in, and thus diminishes the energy in us available for other matters. But there is a device in our minds that comes to our rescue, a kind of Game we play with ourselves. When an impasse goes on for a long time, and we feel we can't bear the anxiety any more, our minds find *phoney solutions* in the form of *contaminations* of the relevant ego states.

When the Parent and Adult become contaminated (that is, they overlap rather than being healthily contiguous), the overlap is *prejudice.*

Consider a man whose Parent ego state contains the belief, 'All Black people are stupid,' (Some people are indoctrinated with some pretty nasty beliefs – see Hitler.) Now this man has a Black neighbour who is highly intelligent and is, indeed, a professor of philosophy at London University. What does the man do with his Parent belief in its contest with the (Adult) reality of his highly intelligent Black neighbour? Well, ideally, his Parent and Adult would have a conversation, and his Parent would acknowledge that the belief he has been taught is false, and he would say to himself something like, 'I used to believe that all Black people were stupid, but the evidence now before me proves that this is false, so I will no longer have this belief.' In principle, it is possible to update our Parent beliefs and values, in the light of experience, but, in practice, it is very difficult to truly cast off any values or beliefs we were given by our parents and teachers when we were children. So what this man is likely to do is tell himself some rubbish like, 'My Black neighbour is very intelligent, but he's the exception that proves the rule.' (see Figure 4.3), which satisfies neither his Parent nor Adult reality, but gives him the illusion that he has solved the problem, thus *relieving himself of anxiety.*

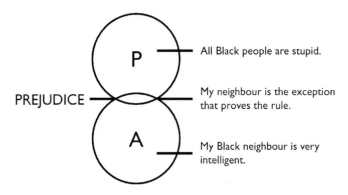

Figure 4.3 Prejudice

But not only has he not solved the problem, he has invested even more energy in the contamination than he had done in the original (honest and therefore healthy) impasse, more locked-in energy that is not available for use elsewhere. He needs to invest this extra energy in the contamination in order to barricade himself his own awareness and other people's exposure of the sham of his created prejudice. This is the price he pays for the reduction of his anxiety. (In everyday parlance, we might say that somebody who believes 'All Black people are stupid' is itself an expression of a prejudice, but, technically, it is just a belief, which only becomes a prejudice when the person continues to hold that belief in the face of contrary (Adult) facts that he or she encounters.)

Now consider a contamination that I have many times been guilty of falling into. I go into a shop and covet a dress that my Child wants badly, but it is very expensive, and my Parent promptly reminds me that I have my electricity and council tax bills to pay; that is, I can't afford the dress. I try it on and take it off, and try it on again, and still want it very badly. Eventually, I decide, 'To hell with the electricity and council tax bills, I'm going to let my Child have its way.' So I go to the counter and pay for it and, as I am already loaded with shopping, I ask for it to be delivered to my home. The next day, the store phones me and says they are sorry, but they can't deliver the dress to me because I have put next year's date on the cheque. (Figure 4.4). I have achieved nothing through my *confusion* but a short-lived and phoney reduction of anxiety; the *conflict* remains unresolved.

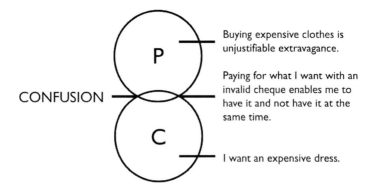

CONFUSION

Buying expensive clothes is unjustifiable extravagance.

Paying for what I want with an invalid cheque enables me to have it and not have it at the same time.

I want an expensive dress.

Figure 4.4 Confusion

As an example of the third kind of contamination, *delusion*, consider a teenage girl who is in love (Child) with a boy and, of course, wants him to be in love with her too. The Adult reality is that not only is the boy not in love with her, but he hardly knows she exists. She goes to a party one night, and the boy is there, at the other side of the room, and he never even comes over to say hello to her, for the whole evening. Out of her Child's *despair*, the next day she says to her best friend, 'He must be in love with me, or he wouldn't have ignored me the way he did last night.' (Figure 4.5)

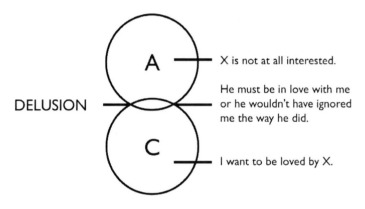

Figure 4.5 Delusion

So how do we break up these contaminations? What we can do, if we are in a relationship with somebody who is chronically locked in a contamination, is to attack it by bombarding it with the energy of the person's *third* ego state, the one not involved in the contamination. In this way, we pull the contaminated ego states apart, and make them face each other again, in their original impasse, and this time find an honest resolution. So, for example, we might say to the man with the *prejudice* about Black people, something like, 'How would you *feel* (Child) if somebody talked like that about you?' For me, in the dress shop, if I had one of my daughters with me, she might say something like, 'Well, look Mum, what about putting a deposit on the dress so they'll hold it for you, and you can pay it off over a few weeks?' (Adult) And, in the case of the girl in love with the boy who barely knows she exists, her friend might say something like, 'Him! You can do much better than that. There are plenty more fish in the sea more worthy of you.' (Parent) So if we experience people we know well who are chronically locked in a contamination, we can help them in these ways. It is unlikely to work instantly, but if you keep on, in a regular way, attacking the contamination with the other, uninvolved ego state, you may, in due course, enable them to resolve their issue healthily.

Uncaring, Turbulent, and Joyless People

When, for whatever reason – innate, conditioned, or circumstantial – even a contamination does not work to allay pain or anxiety, there is a more forceful way our minds work to diminish that pain or anxiety; that is, to completely *repress* the issue out of consciousness. When somebody does this, their aim is only to repress the particular anxiety they are unable to cope with, but unfortunately, it is pragmatically not possible to repress just part of an ego state. When we repress a chunk of an ego state that contains unresolved anxiety, we inevitably repress the whole of that ego state, and we are left with a debilitated capacity for responding to life appropriately.

So when, for whatever reason, somebody has sufficient anxiety in their Parent, and a contamination is not adequate to resolve it, and they take the more radical step of repressing it, they are effectively left with only a functioning Adult and Child. Such an individual is observed by other people to be an *uncaring person*.

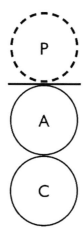

Figure 4.6 The uncaring person

Somebody who has repressed their Adult ego state is likely to be observed as a *turbulent person,* in extreme cases having a bipolar/manic-depressive illness.

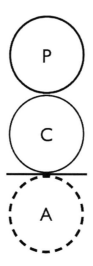

Figure 4.7 The turbulent person

And somebody who has repressed their Child ego state, will be observe tobe a *joyless person.*

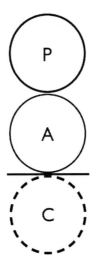

Figure 4.8 The joyless person

Infantile, Cold, and Harsh or Smothering People

Should neither a contamination nor the repression of one ego state suffice to relieve a person of his or her pain or anxiety, the is an even more desperate method our minds may deploy, namely, the effective *repression of two ego states*, clearly leading to a crippling incapacity to cope effectively with everyday life.

If somebody has repressed both Parent and Adult, and is effectively all Child, they are as vulnerable as a baby. By accident, or on purpose, somebody operating only from their Child, and thus unprotected from their own impulses, will die in no time at all, unless there is somebody around to look after them. They will be observed as being *infantile*.

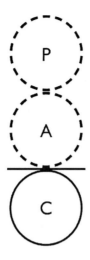

Figure 4.9 The infantile person

Somebody who is effectively only operating from their Adult will be observed as being a *cold person.*

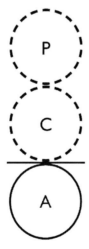

Figure 4.10 The cold person

And somebody who is effectively only operating from Parent will be observed as being either a *smothering* or a *harshly critical person*, depending on the contents of that person's Parent. (In everyday life, it is often difficult to distinguish between the nurturing and critical/controlling functions of the Parent ego state. Consider, for example, a mother shouting at a toddler, 'Don't you ever, ever go near the road,' in which nurture and control are obviously combined.)

Figure 4.11 The harsh or smothering person

Return to Healthy Functioning

At each stage of the process from impasse to contamination to the effective repression out of consciousness of one or two ego states, anxiety diminishes. That is why our minds deploy these unhealthy devices. The paradox is that the more anxious somebody is, the closer they are to healthy functioning. So, very often, when people consult a therapist in a state of acute anxiety, the therapist takes this as a good sign that there is not much work to be done to restore the person to functional health; they are probably locked in an *impasse* and, like a wound up jack-in-a-box, just need a couple more turns of their handle for the lid to burst open, and the problem resolved.

But when somebody has effectively repressed two ego states,

it is extremely difficult to get them even to accept that they have any problem at all, even though those around them are acutely aware that they do. As a psychotherapist, I have, from time to time, had men come to me who are effectively operating only from their Adult. They say, 'I don't know why I'm here. I don't think there's anything wrong with me, but my wife/girlfriend says if I don't get therapy she'll leave me.' Then I have to struggle to drag such a man's Child and Parent back into consciousness, maybe going through contaminations again, then breaking them up, bringing them back to the original impasses, and resolving these through honest confrontation.

The processes from contamination to health are: from (Parent/Adult) prejudice to indecisiveness, to judgement; from (Parent/Child) confusion to conflict, to compromise; and from (Adult/Child) delusion to frustration or despair, to creative alternatives. As such a process gets under way in therapy, the person's anxiety will inevitably increase, as the repressed issues are brought back into consciousness, which accounts for the psychotherapeutic cliché, 'You've got to get worse before you get better.' But the bound energy thus released is worthy of the pain of this healing process.

Chapter Five

From Birth to Maturity

At every moment of our lives, our overall response to our situation and to other people is informed by three contexts: the unchanging attributes or our humanity; our age; and our individuality. The relative influence of each of these contexts may vary although, broadly speaking, our age, - that is, our 'stage of development' – tends to predominate in childhood, our individuality in our middle years, and, ideally, as we grow old, the spirituality associated with our humanity, especially in our coming to terms with ageing and death.

I hope that this chapter will be useful to readers who have children of their own or who work with children, because for all children their given stage of development is very pertinent to their present experience of life and their stroke needs.

Birth to One Year

When we are born we have only one ego state, which is called the Natural Child, designated C_1. Although anybody who has ever visited a maternity ward of a hospital can verify, there are obvious innate temperamental differences between babies – some are peaceful and quiet, others are colicky and wakeful – by and large, all newborn babies are pretty much alike. They scream when they are in pain or hungry, and they are content when they are asleep or suckling. We infer that they have no sense of self, themselves and the universe being one entity.

Gradually, the Natural Child gives away some of its energy to the other emerging ego states, and by the time we are about six years old, the totality of our psychic energy, originally all contained in our Natural Child, is distributed amongst all our now developed ego states.

From when a baby is about six months of age, its behaviour leads us to infer that it is beginning to have a primitive sense of selfhood, beginning to know that its own body is a separate entity from the rest of the world. We infer this from the evidence of such behaviour as the baby throwing its rattle over the side of its cot for Mummy to pick up and give it back, for it to throw it out again ... Or, sucking its own toes, it seems to be thinking, 'This toe is me, but this rattle is not me,' and so on. Certainly by the age of about eight months, when most infants, for the first time, manifest 'separation anxiety', they indicate their achieved awareness of the separateness of themselves from their mothers (or primary caretakers) and their excruciating dependence on her. So a baby who, up until about eight months of age, may have quite happily been bandied about from one adult to another, suddenly will start screaming blue murder if Mummy disappears out of sight, for even a moment, or if he is handed over to a stranger. His primitive sense of 'I' emerges at this time, together with awareness of his vulnerability and his utter dependence on others for his survival.

At the same time, the infant is beginning to acquire some knowledge of a factual kind, but this is not in terms that we consider rational knowledge. Her knowledge is of an intuitive kind, expressed through her newly emerging ego state, the Adult-in-the-Child, designated A_1. This new ego state is *intuition*, and is colloquially called the Little Professor because of its insightful canniness. The Little Professor is the *precursor of the true Adult ego state.* Later on, the Little Professor will be a very important part of the child's (and grown-up's) capacity for creative thinking. It is at this stage that the child begins to be 'cute', that is, she is able to manipulate others with coyness, getting what she wants by smiles and other covert means. (And this is the age when older children in the family begin to be jealous of the baby for her newfound ability to charm adults into giving her what she wants.)

The two now existing ego states, the Natural Child (C_1) and the Little Professor (A_1) together are called the Free Child, because they do not need any encouragement to emerge; we are biologically programmed for them to develop, just as they do in other primate species. Figure 5.1 is a picture of the child's existent ego states at about one year of age. (In this and subsequent diagrams of the ego states, there is no precise quantification of comparative energy levels of the different ego states; they are just qualitative, descriptive diagrams.)

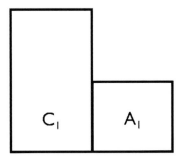

Figure 5.1. Six months to one year

One to Three

By the time the child is about one year old it becomes absolutely essential, in the name of the child's safety and socialization, that the impulses of the Free Child be restrained. In the first year of a child's life, good parents do their best to satisfy more or less all the impulses of the infant. But by the time the child is about one year old, beginning to walk and talk, and to have a clearly emerging sense of 'I', together with autonomous action, parents are neither willing nor able to satisfy all his or her demands. They increasingly need to be able to turn their backs on the child, even if only briefly, confident that the child will not do anything self-destructive or otherwise intolerable to the parents. And in response to the constraints that parents impose on their child, especially between the ages of about one and three years of age, a new ego state emerges, called the Adapted Child and designated P_1. (Other species also have an Adapted Child ego state which, in the case of domestic pets, is largely inculcated by their owners.) The Adapted Child is *the precursor of the true Parent ego state*. The whole Child ego state (C_2) is now complete, being comprised of the Natural Child (C_1), the Little Professor (A_1), and the Adapted Child (P_1).

Between one and three years of age, the true Adult ego state (A_2) also emerges and grows rapidly, especially through language, which epitomizes the functioning Adult more than any other behaviour. The child's Adult is also learning how to build a tower of blocks, blow her nose, eat with a fork and spoon, draw with a crayon, and express multitudinous other practical skills and her acquired knowledge of the world.

The Adapted Child (P_1) is, by definition, in conflict with the impulses of the Free Child, because both the Natural Child (C_1) and the Little Professor (A_1) just impulsively want to express themselves, to do what they want and get what they want, without any regard for safety or consideration of others. So all the parents' communications that inform the child's Adapted Child begin with 'Don't'. The Adapted Child is grown by the necessary *inculcation of fear.* 'Don't pull the cat's tail, don't pick your nose, don't scream, but ask politely, don't go near the road or the fire, don't tear my books, don't scribble on the walls ...' All of these Don'ts are vitally necessary at this stage of the child's development, so that parents and caretakers can turn their backs for a moment, confident that the child will not immediately put her life at risk, and so that they can take the child out in public and have her behave in an acceptable way in the world at large. And all these Don'ts have to be imposed with a loud voice and a frowning expression on the part of the parents, *frightening the child into obedience.* Thus an appropriately conditioned eighteen-month old child might be in a room on his own, with a fire, Mummy having left the room for a few minutes, confident that the child will not touch the fire. He may walk very close to it, then stop in his tracks, shaking his head in imitation of Mummy, and saying to himself, 'No, no. Naughty. Don't go near fire.' Quite naturally, between the ages of one and three, the child wants, above all else, to please Mummy and Daddy. It is the stage of development associated with the control of impulse in general and, notwithstanding that children in this age group do have defiant temper-tantrums, on balance they are compliant, and quite often even say, 'Am I being good, Mummy?'

All the Don'ts that are imposed on us at this stage of our development are received as *imperatives we are likely to obey for the rest of our lives*, in contrast to the instructions we later receive into our growing Parent ego state, which may be modified in adult life through our own experiences and meetings with admired others. The one-to-three year old does not have a Parent ego state to justify – nor a sufficiently developed Adult to rationalize – why Don'ts are imposed; he merely accepts them as rigid and binding rules. Thus most grown-ups continue always to say please and thank you, to look both ways before crossing the road, and continue to be obedient to all the other constraints imposed on them when they were between one and three years of age. (Indeed, so ingrained are our Adapted Child inhibitions that, for example, many grown-ups find it impossible to cross a road without looking both ways first, even when they are fully aware of it as being a one-way street.)

Most of the prohibitions that parents instil into the Adapted Child of the one-to-three year old are very life-preserving and socializing. And, throughout our lives, if we disobey the prohibitions in our Adapted Child, we will feel some kind of target negative stroke, we will feel bad in some way. So the problem is, from the parents' point of view, to make prohibitive only those things that are really necessary in the name of the child's safety and socialization. But, unfortunately, all of us, being sons and daughters of Adam and Eve and cast out of paradise, have hang-ups, which are transmitted down the generations via the Adapted Child. Willy-nilly, with the best will in the world, all parents will transmit – more often covertly, by facial expressions and mannerisms, than by direct exhortation – prohibitions which are quite unnecessary, and which are, broadly speaking, the neurotic components of our personalities. And it is these that are expressed through the roles of Persecutor, Rescuer, and Victim, when we play Games, and which are parts of the Adapted Child of all of us.

(For the record, there are five broad types of bad feelings we give ourselves in obedience to our neurotic Adapted Child prohibitions. They are: Don't feel good about yourself; Don't feel loveworthy; Don't express bad feelings; Don't succeed; and Don't belong. We probably all have some of each of them in our Adapted Childs, but we are distinguished as individuals by the hierarchy of these prohibitions in the structure of our personalities. And while each of these prohibitions causes pain in our lives, they are also the basis of all the accomplishments of human kind. For those readers who would like to pursue this subject, it is elaborated in my books *How to Choose a Mate* and *Pain & Joy in Intimate Relationships*.)

By the time we are three years old, we have a complete Child ego state (C_2), and an Adult ego state (A_2) emerging in leaps and bounds.

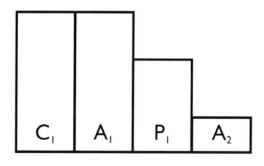

Figure 5.2. One to three

Three to Six

Between three and six years of age, we experience the famous Oedipal state of development which, psychoanalytically speaking, is the last stage in the formation of our lifelong personality and character. This is the stage when the true Parent ego state (P_2) emerges, through the following scenario. Every little boy falls in love with Mummy, and wishes Daddy out of the way so he can 'marry' Mummy. But he has to come to terms with the realization that he can't have Mummy because she already belongs to Daddy, and he doesn't really want to get rid of Daddy because he quite likes Daddy, and Daddy is quite useful, anyhow. So, by the end of this stage of development, at about six years of age, the little boy has formed a *compromise* (between his Child and his Parent), along the lines of, 'I can't have Mummy, because she already belongs to Daddy, so when I'm grown up I'll be a man *like* Daddy, and marry a lady *like* Mummy. Conversely, the little girl of this age decides, 'I can't have Daddy, because he already belongs to Mummy, so when I'm grown up I'll be a lady *like* Mummy, and marry a man *like* Daddy. (We seem to be hardwired for this experience, and there is considerable evidence that, in the absence of a parent in the life of a child at this stage of development, the child will fantasize that parent, and use that fantasy as a necessary protagonist in his or her own Oedipal story.)

There is, though, some asymmetry in the experiences of boys and girls at this stage of their development. Typically, both boys and girls spend a great deal more time with their mothers (and other women, such as nursery school teachers) than they spend with their fathers (and other men). This probably accounts for men's greater dependency on women, throughout their lives, than women's dependency on men, despite men's well-known 'commitment phobia' protest. But that's just my opinion!

Out of the 'Oedipal triangle' of mother, father, and child locked into the intense feelings of love and rivalry, together with the child's first real understanding of gender differences (which becomes a giggling matter), the child becomes *emotionally literate*. By about six years of age, we have all experienced the whole range of human emotions: love, hate, jealousy, rivalry, disappointment, rage, competitiveness, aggression, tenderness ... The only thing yet to be experienced is full genital sexuality, the capacity for which will not be developed for about another eight years.

Our acquired Parent ego state is our *character*; the totality of our Child is our *personality*.

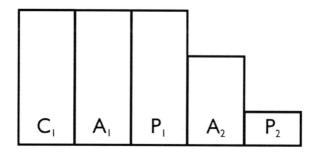

Figure 5.3. Three to six

Between three and six years of age is a good time for a child to acquire a baby brother or sister, desirous as he now is to practise the skills of his emergent Parent. And youngest children in a family benefit similarly by acquiring a pet at this stage of their development.

One of the most valuable aspects of the development of our Parent is that we can now understand the justifications for all the Adapted Child restrictions that were earlier imposed on us. It is at this stage that good parents expend the time and energy necessary for explanations that enable the growing child to acquire a degree of *flexibility*, which the Adapted Child never has. For example, think of a two-and-a-half year old child who has been told, 'You must never ever eat chocolate after bathtime,' so the child never eats chocolate after bathtime, but has no idea why. Should he disobey that inhibition, he will feel very bad about himself. At two-and-a-half, he is incapable of understanding that he is not allowed to eat chocolate after this time because he has just cleaned his teeth, that chocolate contains sugar, etc. ...

But consider a five-year-old whose parents have explained to her why she is not allowed to have chocolate after cleaning her teeth. The child now understands it has to do with sugar and tooth decay, etc. Let's say that, on one occasion, this five-year-old has had her bath and cleaned her teeth, and then Auntie Flo comes to visit with a box of chocolates. The child is now capable of saying, 'Mummy, Auntie Flo has offered me a chocolate. Can I have one if I promise to clean my teeth again, afterwards?' thereby demonstrating her ability to obey the spirit, rather than just the letter, of the law

Furthermore, the emotional maturity of the five-year-old is such that she is capable of sometimes understanding and telling a 'white lie'. So if Auntie Flo gives her a present she doesn't like, she doesn't say, 'Yuk,' but rather, 'Thank you, Auntie Flo, it's lovely,' thus demonstrating her *taught* awareness that, although truthfulness and kindness are both moral (Parent) values, when push comes to shove kindness comes somewhat above truth. Such awareness demonstrates the emotional sophistication already achieved by a five or six-year old.

Before the age of about four or five, any apparently Parent behaviour on the part of a child, such as 'helping Mummy' or 'sharing chocolate with her dolly', is only *imitative Adapted Child behaviour*, unrelated to any true caring for or sharing with others. She will 'help Mummy' for a minute, and then walk through the dirt she has swept up; and she will 'eat Dolly's chocolate for her.' Pre-emptively making a child under the age of four or five share his or her toys, for example, will only make the child, later, much more possessively *unsharing* of her possessions, because she has not been allowed the natural stage of learning respect for other people's possessions, and reciprocally having her own rights of possession respected. Indeed, the willingness of any of us, as grown-ups, to share our possessions is very limited and only possible because of our understanding that, in order for others ever to be willing to be kind and generous towards us, they need to know that we will sometimes be kind and generous to them also. True altruism is very rare. *Compromise* is what civilization is about.

Six Years Old

At six years of age our personalities (C_2) and character (P_2) are complete and, for a brief period, not to be reiterated for another fifteen or twenty years, when functional maturity is attained, we have all our ego states operating well and in harmony with each other. Thus the six-year-old is every reception teacher's delight.

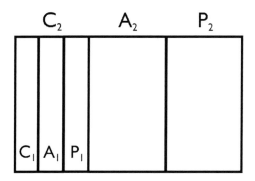

Figure 5.4 Six years old

Six to Twelve

Nature cooperates with culture by precipitating the Adult into dominance during this stage of development. It is the stage called 'latency' by Freud, referring to the fact that sexuality is latent. The years between three and six have been very sexual (albeit non-genitally so), as will life again be from puberty onwards. But, for the time being, the focus is on acquiring literacy and numeracy and other skills, especially including how to get on well with our same-sexed peers, which is a necessary preliminary to our learning competence in our relationships with the opposite sex. Though latent, heterosexual impulses by no means disappear, and most of us have memories of 'I'll show you mine if you show me yours' behind the bike shed during this stage of our development. Nevertheless, the dominant theme of this stage is the acquisition of many competencies in relation to the impersonal world . This stage can be usefully thought of as a repetition, at a higher level, of the six to twelve-month old stage, when the Little Professor (A_1) was dominant in its development. Then, the infant learnt, through knocks and bumps and scratches, the power of the material world, towards which he had to learn respect. Now, he wants to demonstrate his own power and control over the environment.

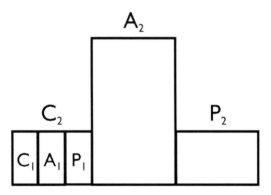

Figure 5.5. Six to twelve

Much of the rearing of the child at this stage is handed over to teachers, with most parents offering the child lots of additional Adult-oriented extras, such as music and swimming lessons, outings to museums, etc. This is a very sensible age because it is so Adult dominated. But, notwithstanding the emotional respite it gives parents after the challenges of the pre-school years and before the onslaught of puberty, the child can be quite boring in his factual orientation, such as recounting every single frame of a film he has just seen and often insistently 'starting again, because you haven't been listening.'

By virtue of the dominance of the Adult at this stage, it is the time when children are best able to cope with emotionally stressful circumstances. Many parents, if they are unhappily married, mistakenly believe that the older the child is the better able he or she will be able to cope with their divorce. This is not the case. Ages three to six and all of the teenage years are the most emotionally vulnerable stages of life; so, if needs must, it is wiser for parents to choose to separate when their children are aged between six and twelve.

The only major problem the child has to endure during this stage of development is her now fully realistic awareness of death – its irreversibility, and the fact that everybody, including her parents and herself, will one day die. Sometimes, the child's fear of death is expressed openly, but most often it is defended against by obsessive-compulsive behaviour, which is a magical way of 'stopping bad things happening', the ultimate 'bad thing' being death. Thus the child seeks, as it were, to be in control of the universe, by superstitious actions, such as always or never stepping on the lines of the pavement, creating perfect order in her possessions of stamps, badges and certificates of merit, etc. One of the ways in which boys, in particular, defend themselves against the fear of death is by playing, 'Bang, bang, you're dead' games, in which the victim is bound to fall down; but then, of course, the 'dead' rise again and the game continues. Girls are usually more likely to act out the same impulse in more indirect ways, by verbal viciousness and excluding (killing off) those they don't want in their 'gangs'.

I recall that my younger daughter, when she was about ten, began compulsively touching doorknobs a certain number of times, every time she entered or left a room. I could see that it was an obsessive-compulsive ritual she had superstitiously impose d on herself, and I let it go on, not wanting to shame her with my awareness of what she was doing. But eventually the number of times she had to touch doorknobs increased to the point that she was making herself late for school; the anxiety she was inducing in herself was outstripping the reassurance her behaviour was designed to achieve. I realized some intervention was needed. I had an idea that I wasn't sure would work, but decided to give it a go. One night, as she was going to bed, I said, 'You know how you have to touch doorknobs a lot? Is it to stop bad things happening?' Somewhat shamefacedly, she said, 'Yes.'

'Well,' I said, 'I'll tell you why. It's because a long time ago a wicked witch cast a spell on you. Now the only people whose spells are more powerful than witches' are mothers' so, when I say abracadabra three times, the spell will be broken, and you'll never have to touch doorknobs again, and nothing bad will happen! Her face lit up with immense relief, and it worked, I'm glad to say – like a charm! It only worked because, although her ten-year old Adult knew what I was saying was nonsense, her Child so desperately wanted that magic to work that she disenfranchised her Adult, by repressing it out of consciousness, and allowed her frightened Child to be healed. The role I was able to play with my daughter is the role that grown-ups, having realized that Mummy and Daddy are, after all, not omnipotent, ascribe to God, the super-duper Parent, who makes everything all right in the end.

Twelve to Sixteen

At puberty, between about twelve and sixteen, the Adapted Child is paramount again, as it was between one and three years of age. And, of course, the Natural Child is also dominant, in the form of all those hormones that come rushing in, and play havoc with the lives of pubescents and their parents. All the Adapted Child 'Don'ts' now become 'Do's'; the child behaves with an insistent absence of good manners, and has hare-brained disregard for his own safety and anything that implies submitting to the wishes of his parents. This is the necessary counterbalance to the earlier, essentially compliant, stage between one and three. The Adapted Child has a compliant *and* a defiant side and, unless both have been played out, the child cannot proceed to full maturity in his Parent. It is only the mature, true Parent that can say, 'Sometimes I am wrong, and then I will apologize; and sometimes I will find you wrong, and then I will blame you.' The fully developed Parent is the successor to the Adapted Child which, as it were, practises an immature morality, by being either wholly compliant or wholly defiant, in rigid, unjustified ways. If the defiant phase of the Adapted Child is not played out at puberty, the Parent ego state cannot achieve full maturity.

At this stage, the child's Parent is virtually decommissioned. Teachers do their best to keep the Adult going, stroking it up with the promise of GCSEs and qualifications, even though their task is very difficult. And, to the child, parents are just ogres and prison warders on whom, she poignantly realizes, she is still dependent, especially for money. The pubescent now appreciates money in the same way as adults do, and both boys and girls want it – and lots of it – for sexual display purposes and status – clothes, make-up, the latest i-Pad, etc. This gives parents their only real power at this stage, the giving and withholding of money. For the time being, bribery is a parent's own best survival technique.

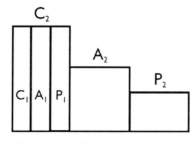

Figure 5.6 Twelve to sixteen

Yet, underneath all his defiance, the pubescent still wants his parents' approval and control, although he'll never admit it. The unhappiest pubescents are those whose parents have effectively 'given up', and allow their children unbridled expression of their wild and amoral Free Childs and their (defiant) Adapted Childs.

Sixteen Plus

This, adolescence, is the final stage of child development, which is often not complete until the mid-to late-twenties. At this time, the three-to-six-year old Oedipal stage of development is being recapitulated, with the child now being physiologically sexually mature. So, although by this stage the Adult ego state has been reinstated and 'stroked up' with some academic achievement, and the child is showing some intelligent interest in matters beyond the instantaneous gratification of his Child impulses, family life is still fraught.

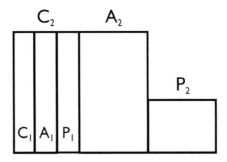

Figure 5.7 Adolescence: Sixteen plus

This is the stage when the Parent ego state gets polished up, enabling the young adult to go out into the world, well-armed with a useful set of values and moral precepts, enabling her to function competently away from the protection and control of her parents.

Children now know they still need their parents but, consciously or unconsciously, they are bound to keep their distance from their opposite-sexed parent, in the name of avoiding breaching the incest taboo. And they also need to keep an antagonistic distance from their same-sexed parent, towards whom they feel rivalrous inferiority with regard to the sexual experience and many other competencies the parent has, which they themselves have not yet achieved. So the opposite-sexed parent makes him- or herself as scarce as possible in the adolescent's life; and the same-sexed parent walks on eggshells, down-playing his or her own attractiveness and competencies, out of regard for the adolescent's still fragile self-esteem.

But the child inevitably feels humiliated by her continuing dependence, which she defends herself against with a prideful Game. With her now well-developed Adult, she launches a two-pronged attack on her parents' Adult and Parent ego states, with supreme rationality, avowing her freedom to have sex with whomever she feels like, to come home whenever she feels like it, to not come to visit her grandparents next Sunday, to never go to church again, etc. etc.

Wise parents know that, notwithstanding the child's stated revulsion towards them, and his unwillingness to adhere to their moral precepts, he still needs the strength of their Parental control. The prideful Game the adolescent is playing is shown in Figure 5.8.

Nominally and overtly, the adolescent is declaring his autonomy, but covertly his still under-developed Parent is begging his parents' Parents to show their strength under attack, and *not* to crumble, so allowing him to internalize their Parent strength and take it with him, out into the grown-up world. So wise parents avoid getting hooked into the nominal 'rational' (Adult) debate the adolescent invites them into. Instead, they respond from their Parent with, 'Yes, I know I can't stop you having sex but, whether you like it or not, so long as you live under my roof, you are *not* going to bring your boyfriend home to sleep with you, you *are* coming to visit your grandparents next

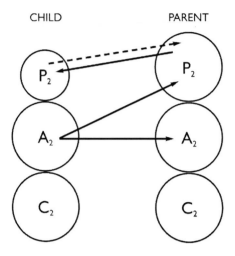

Figure 5.8 The Game adolescents play

Sunday. You'll just have to accept that I know better than you what is right and wrong, which has nothing whatsoever to do with rational debate ...' etc. etc. The adolescent is actually deeply grateful, although he is unlikely to admit it until he is well-established in adult life and is probably a parent himself.

Although all of our ego states make up our 'total self', when people ordinarily talk about 'self-confidence' they are almost always referring to a confident Parent ego state, that is, the convinced assurance with which people express their values and beliefs and moral code, even in the face of opposition. Creating this in the adolescent is the final responsibility of good parents in the rearing of their children.

Maturity

Finally, we achieve the recapitulation of our delightful six-year old selves, with all our ego states harmoniously represented and expressed, now in their full maturity. By this time, adolescents have probably lost their virginity and thereby gained considerable self-esteem. So they no longer feel the threat (however unconscious) of their incestuous impulses towards their opposite-sexed parent; nor do they any longer feel humiliatingly inferior to their same-sexed parent. Peace is restored to the family and – at least in principle – the child can again enjoy asexual loving intimacy with both parents, which they all last experienced before the child was three years old.

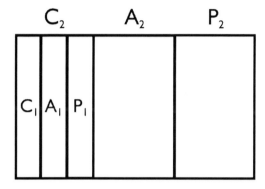

Figure 5.9. Maturity

Appendix: About Transactional Analysis

Transactional Analysis (or TA as it is familiarly called) is the creation of the Canadian-born psychiatrist, Eric Berne (1910-70).

In 1956, after more than a decade of being in a training analysis, the San Francisco Psychoanalytic Institute rejected Berne's application for certification as a psychoanalyst, deeming him 'not ready'. This failure intensified his long-standing ambition to add something new to psychoanalysis, and he was now determined to 'show them' with a completely new approach to psychotherapy.

The essential disagreement between Berne and establishment psychoanalysis concerned practice, not theory. He was, and remained all his life, committed to orthodox psychoanalytic theory, but his frustration with the slowness of psychoanalysis, as therapy, to effect measurable change in his patients made him baulk at the overly passive role demanded of the analyst. He questioned the assumptions behind the procedures of psycho-analysis as therapy, and he decided that, in one respect, they were false. Where psychoanalysis insisted that unconscious conflicts must be resolved before manifest personality changes could effectively and permanently achieved, Berne claimed that patients could be made better *first* – and quickly – and have their underlying conflicts resolved later (if required). Thus, out of a practical concern to cure people quickly, TA came into being, and developed as a theoretical elaboration of psychoanalytic ego psychology and a systematized approach to ego therapy.

What distinguishes TA from other theoretical elaborations of the ego is that its concepts are direct derivatives of psycho-analysis as a whole. The Parent, Adult, and Child ego states are exact derivatives of the superego, ego, and id, but describe the here-and-nowness of our conscious lives. What Berne proposed was essentially Freud without the unconscious.

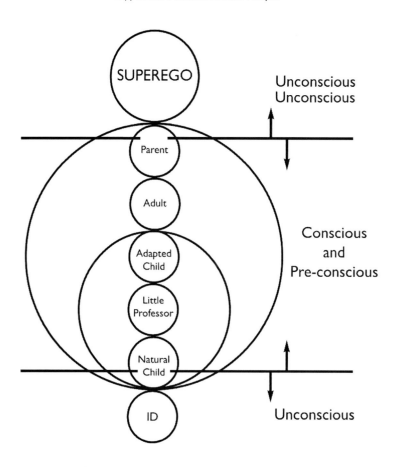

The Psychoanalytic and TA Models of the Mind Combined

Berne realized that the core existential reality of any human being is accessible through the conscious and pre-conscious ego, and can be revealed by a skilled psychotherapist in a few hours rather than a few years!

This is so, argued Berne, because the experiences we have in the later stages of our development are, through the influence of the 'repetition compulsion', very similar to the primary experiences of the first six years of our lives. And, unlike the repressed experiences of our earliest years (which can take years to tease into consciousness), our most significant experiences after the age of six are available to our pre-conscious minds and can quickly be brought into full consciousness.

The concept of the ego states and the delineation of their natures is undoubtedly the central genius of TA theory and therapy. But what makes TA more than 'psychoanalysis without the unconscious' is its concept of strokes, for which TA is indebted to 'operant conditioning', the learning theory of the behaviourist psychologist, B. F. Skinner. Thus TA is a highly successful marriage of the most unlikely bedfellows, psychoanalysis and behaviourism. It is both 'hard' and 'soft', diagnostic and prescriptive, subjective and objective, holistic and atomistic, and its basic concepts are so easily understood that they can be communicated with ease to even very young children.

Eric Berne wrote six books on TA, beginning with *Transactional Analysis in Psychotherapy,* first published in 1961, and culminating in *What Do You Say After You Say Hello?* published posthumously in 1970. *Games People Play*, published in 1964, became a worldwide bestseller, and the concept of 'playing games' has permeated everyday language, and is at least vaguely understood and referred to by people who have never even heard of Transactional Analysis.

Since January 1971, the official organ of the International Transactional Analysis Association (headquarters in San Francisco) has been the quarterly *Transactional Analysis Journal*, in whose pages TA theory and application have continued to evolve. Many important concepts now familiarly used by TA therapists and teachers were only incipient in *What Do You Say After You Say Hello?* but fortunately there have been many brilliant followers of Berne, in whose minds these ideas have germinated and been brought to life. (The explications of ego state contaminations and exclusions, in Chapter 4 of this book, are amongst my own contributions to evolving TA theory.)

As well as being a very popular form of humanistic psychotherapy, TA is now widely taught in educational and business settings throughout the world. The British Institute of Transactional Analysis was the first TA organization to be formed outside the United States, in 1974, followed by the formation of the European Association for Transactional Analysis (EATA), in 1975. Both are still flourishing.

Glossary

ADAPTED CHILD. That part of the CHILD EGO STATE which is learned, as contrasted with the FREE CHILD, which is innate. The Adapted Child is acquired mostly between the ages of about one and three, in the form of rigid rules restricting expression of the FREE CHILD. Its function is to ensure self-preservation. It is the precursor of the PARENT EGO STATE, which develops between the ages of three and six.

ADULT. The EGO STATE that contains knowledge and skills. It first appears in the 'whole self' at about one year of age, and it grows most rapidly from then until about three years of age, and again between the ages of about six and twelve, although it is capable of continued growth throughout life. Its function in the 'whole self' is to store, process, and access information it receives from the environment, and to make sense of life by reconciling its own information with the values of the PARENT EGO STATE and the feelings of the CHILD EGO STATE.

ALTERNATIVES. The outcome of the effective collaboration of the ADULT and CHILD EGO STATES.

CHARACTER. The contents and behaviour of the PARENT EGO STATE.

CHILD. The EGO STATE that contains and expresses our feelings and impulses, both innate and conditioned. It consists of the NATURAL CHILD, the LITTLE PROFESSOR, and the ADAPTED CHILD.

COMPROMISE. The outcome of the effective collaboration of the PARENT and CHILD EGO STATES.

CONFLICT. The experience of an IMPASSE between the PARENT and CHILD EGO STATES.

CONFUSION. The content of the CONTAMINATION of the PARENT and CHILD EGO STATES.

CONTAMINATION. A maladaptive, pseudo-resolution of an IMPASSE between EGO STATES, in which the incompatible impulses or attitudes of the relevant EGO STATES are expressed in a single, inauthentic idea or attitude.

DELUSION. The content of the CONTAMINATION of the ADULT AND CHILD EGO STATES.

DRAMA TRIANGLE. A simple diagram illustrating the roles of PERSECUTOR, RESCUER, and VICTIM, amongst which people move when they are playing GAMES.

EGO STATE. One of the 'sub-selves' that go to make up the 'whole self' of every human being. These are the PARENT, the ADULT, and the CHILD.

EXCLUSION. The dissociation of one of more EGO STATES from a person's everyday functioning.

FREE CHILD. That part of the CHILD EGO STATE which is innate, consisting of the NATURAL CHILD and the LITTLE PROFESSOR (as contrasted with the ADAPTED CHILD, which is conditioned). It contains, and expresses spontaneously, feelings and impulses that are authentic and appropriate to its desires and reactions.

FRUSTRATION. The experience of an IMPASSE between the ADULT and CHILD EGO STATES.

GAME. A set series of inauthentic, ulterior TRANSACTIONS, ending in a NEGATIVE STROKE for both parties.

IMPASSE The experience of an unresolved disagreement between two EGO STATES, when they are equally energized, and neither will give in or make concessions to the other.

INDECISIVENESS. The experience of an IMPASSE between the PARENT AND ADULT EGO STATES.

INTIMACY. A candid, FREE CHILD to FREE CHILD relationship, without ulterior motives, reservations, or exploitation, from which the most valued STROKES are obtained, but which is also associated with the greatest psychological vulnerability.

JUDGEMENT. The outcome of the effective collaboration of the PARENT and ADULT EGO STATES.

LITTLE PROFESSOR. The exploratory part of the CHILD EGO STATE, which develops spontaneously from about six months of age. It is the precursor of the ADULT EGO STATE.

NATURAL CHILD. The innate part of the CHILD EGO STATE, the only EGO STATE of a newborn baby.

PARENT. The EGO STATE that contains our values and beliefs and moral principles and generalizations about life. It is basically formed between the ages of about three and six through explicit exhortations by our parents concerning caring for and controlling ourselves and others. In grown-up life, the Parent is capable of modification and growth, to the extent that we may reject old values and acquire new ones as a consequence of new experiences and meetings with new, admired people. But, by and large, our Parent remains committed to the principles it was taught in early childhood. Its function in the 'whole self' is to enable us automatically to behave in ways which are conducive to our own and others' wellbeing, including the monitoring of our FREE CHILD, by granting it indulgences or imposing constraints, in accordance with the Parent's principles. In its constraining of the FREE CHILD, the Parent often looks like the ADAPTED CHILD, but the Parent acts in accordance with general principles, and may be flexible, whereas the ADAPTED CHILD is utterly rule-bound and rigid.

PERSECUTOR. One of the compulsive, maladaptive roles through which the ADAPTED CHILD EGO STATE expresses itself in a GAME. The Persecutor role is associated with an inauthentic feeling of 'Now I've got you, you son-of-a-bitch.'

PERSONALITY. The contents and behaviour of the CHILD EGO STATE.

PREJUDICE. The content of the CONTAMINATION of the PARENT and ADULT EGO STATES.

RESCUER. One of the compulsive, maladaptive roles through which the ADAPTED CHILD EGO STATE expresses itself in a GAME. The Rescuer role is associated with an inauthentic feeling of self-righteousness.

STROKE. Any act of recognition given by one person to another. Our need for and quest for strokes is continuous and lifelong. When positive strokes – which make us feel good – are not available, we would rather get negative strokes – which make us feel bad – than receive no strokes at all, that is, be ignored. At birth, we are only capable of appreciating the most fundamental strokes, that is, actual physical contact with another human being but, gradually, we learn to value as strokes a wide variety of symbolic substitutes for physical contact, from the slightly valued nod of a passing acquaintance to the profoundly gratifying, 'I love you.' The strokes, both positive and negative, that we were often given us in childhood by our parents are the strokes we are most likely to seek and to get from other people, for the rest of our lives. These, our favourite strokes, are called our 'target strokes'. We each have our own positive and negative target strokes, respectively those that make us feel especially good, and those that make us feel especially bad about ourselves.

STRUGGLE. The experience of an IMPASSE between the ADULT AND CHILD EGO STATES.

TRANSACTION. Any interaction between people, irrespective of whether or not words are spoken. All transactions involve the giving and getting of strokes.

TRILOG. A simple diagram showing how the EGO STATES collaborate to form JUDGEMENTS, ALTERNATIVES, AND COMPROMISES.

VICTIM. One of the compulsive, maladaptive roles through which the ADAPTED CHILD EGO STATE expresses itself in a GAME. The Victim role is associated with an inauthentic feeling of helplessness.

**PSYCHE
BOOKS**

The study of the mind: interactions, behaviours, functions. Developing and learning our understanding of self. Psyche Books cover all aspects of psychology and matters relating to the head.